Hsing-i

To my parents, who always have time to sit and talk. Even in the times of disagreement and difficulty, I have known that they are always on my side.

Special thanks to Erle Montaigue for his brilliance in the internal arts and his constant encouragement.

Untraditional Hsing-i

Secrets of Five-Element Boxing

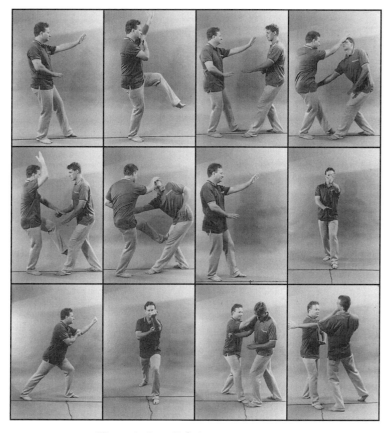

Robb Whitewood

Paladin Press · Boulder, Colorado

Untraditional Hsing-i:
Secrets of Five-Element Boxing
by Robb Whitewood

Copyright © 1999 by Robb Whitewood

ISBN 1-58160-030-5
Printed in the United States of America

Published by Paladin Press, a division of
Paladin Enterprises, Inc., P.O. Box 1307,
Boulder, Colorado 80306, USA.
(303) 443-7250

Direct inquiries and/or orders to the above address.

Visit our Web site at: www.paladin-press.com

A videotape containing all of the movements, patterns, and applications described
in this book is available from www.warriors.com.au. in VHS (U.S. format) and
PAL. The program is also available on CD-ROM. E-mail the author with inquiries
at robb@warriors.com.au.

Contents

Warning

The information and techniques presented herein can be dangerous and could result in serious injury or death. The author, publisher, and distributors of this book disclaim any liability from any damage or injuries of any type that a reader or user of information contained in this book may incur from the use of said information. This book is *for academic study only.*

Foreword

U pon observing me, a student of Sensei Keiji Tomiyama said to him, "But, Sensei, he does not even look like a martial artist." Sensei Tomiyama then said to him that it is the martial artist who does not look like a martial artist or try to be a martial artist from whom you should learn.

A true warrior is one who is not concerned with being a martial artist. He is not concerned with putting others down for the sake of pushing himself forward. A true warrior is one who is concerned with the well-being of others, in particular his students. He is happy when his students excel to the point where they are technically better at the art than he is. He is one who knows about healing as well as self-defense. And most importantly, he is one who does not look like a martial artist.

I have known Robb Whitewood since 1983, and he has all of those qualities that make a true warrior.

His knowledge of hsing-i is great, so much so that he is now the head of hsing-i for my organization, the World Taiji Boxing Association. As with the internal martial arts of t'ai chi and bagwazhang, there has been much rubbish written over the years by those who think that they know martial arts and think that they are martial artists. So when I read Robb Whitewood's manuscript, I was happy with the final product. Robb is an innovator, not afraid to say when something is wrong and change it, never falling into the trap of always believing that an old Chinese master could never be wrong. Always questioning what is taught to him (I know about this from teaching Robb t'ai chi chuan). So it is with great pleasure that I now recommend this book to all martial artists no matter what system you practice. You will gain much knowledge not only of your martial art, but also about yourself.

–Erle Montaigue

Preface

I started training in martial arts at the age of 8. I began with judo in Sydney, then Goju karate in Hong Kong when I was 10. On returning to Australia at age 15, I joined the God Dragon Society in Sydney and started my studies in hsing-i (pronounced shing-yee), pa-kua, and t'ai chi under Dean Rainer and Frank Lee. For the following four or five years I lived in a small van and worked as an apprentice aircraft sheet-metal engineer with Qantas Airways during the day. I would begin my studies at 4 P.M. four nights a week and also teach the Saturday morning class. I slept in the jet base car park so I could save the extra two or three hours a day in travel time.

Not all of my studies involved physical training. Early in the afternoons I would read about Chinese philosophy and acupuncture and help out in the acupuncture and chiropractic clinic, answering the phones and watching the practitioners. At 6:30 P.M., training began. In the beginning, this was just plain hell—45 minutes of a combination of push-ups, squats, sit-ups, side raises, and jumping. It was all done to a count of 10 or sometimes 15, with no rest between exercises. In the beginning it pushed my heart rate to the limit. This was followed by a run of 20 to 25 minutes in bare feet around the streets of inner-city Sydney. Then came more training up and down the floor—elements, kicking, applications, and forms.

Many people came to look at the classes, but few joined. Of those who joined, most only lasted a couple of nights. Understandably, the school was never that big, possibly only 20 to 30 students. The class was made up of two to four instructors, 10 senior students, and some intermediate students and beginners.

In time I came to question why so much physical training was needed. It was not till many years later that I realized the teachers wanted to know if we were serious about our training. It was also invaluable for teaching ease of movement. When most people started to train they fought with the exercises, and, of course, the exercises fought back. The count for the exercises was just fast enough that if you fought them they would always win. In time you simply surrendered to the exercises and the movements just flowed. For me, when the surrender took place it was like magic. Mind you, I was pretty stubborn. It took me nearly three years to get to this point.

As the years passed I ended up doing massages in the clinic and treating simple problems. It was at the beginning of this period that I decided what I wanted to do with my life: to be a practitioner of traditional Chinese medicine and a teacher of hsing-i. This led to three years with Acupuncture Colleges Australia, then to Tokyo for two years, studying with the Institute of Oriental Medicine and at the shrine of Torjinga. During this time I was fortunate to train with Master Yeu Chen, who had been national wu shu coach in mainland

China. The next step in the journey was to Taiwan for clinical studies and then on to England for practitioner certification in neuro linguistic programming (NLP). I returned to Australia to continue studying NLP and also studied hypnosis and Timeline Therapy® to the level of master practitioner.

The reason for all this training and study was to produce a system that married the best of the West with the best of the East. NLP and Timeline Therapy produce a system that can dramatically reduce the amount of time it takes to master an internal system. It is this system that I now teach at the Internal Martial Arts Academy.

Introduction

W hat makes hsing-i so special is its phenomenal speed and power—I am talking about three blocks and three full-power hits in under a second. This may seem like an unbelievable claim, but instructors and senior students in the Internal Martial Arts Academy achieve this on a nightly basis. Hsing-i is, after all, a hitting art. The reasons for this speed and power are not found in any mystical change in body chemistry or prayer to a special martial arts god. It is about simple physics, geometry, neurology, and muscle coordination, put together in a way that only the Chinese mind could do. The bulk of my training has been spent working with hsing-i. The more I learn about hsing-i, the more I realize that its unbelievable power is often hidden by its simplicity of movement.

With this idea of simplicity in mind, I teach hsing-i in an untraditional way. I teach the basics and then move straight to the understanding and application of movements. It has been my experience that Westerners on the whole are far less patient than their Eastern cousins, so the system of hsing-i that I teach is translated for Western minds to take apart and work with.

I learned two important things about translation when I was in Japan teaching English for a couple of years. My first lesson was about the importance of context. Often students would come to class and have a conversation with me in near-perfect English, and I would have no idea what they were talking about. Frequently this was because I was missing a little bit of cultural schema, or context. If you don't think this is important, read the section below:

> This is an easy thing to do. If possible you will do it at home, but you can always go somewhere else if it is necessary. Beware of overdoing it. This is a major mistake and may cost you quite a bit of money. It is far better to do too little than attempt to do too much. Make sure everything is properly placed. Now you are ready to proceed. The next step is put things into another convenient arrangement. Once done you'll probably have to start again real soon. Most likely you'll be doing this for the rest of your life. (*Mega Speed Reading Workbook* by Howard S. Berg)

You probably have absolutely no idea what the passage is talking about. But if you know the schema of the passage—washing clothes—it makes a big difference. The same kind of confusion occurs with most translations of martial arts text into English. This is not done on purpose; it is just that the context is taken for granted by a native speaker of any language.

The second lesson I learned was that words may translate

into a foreign tongue, but concepts don't translate unless there is common experience. At the end of the day a translation from any language to another is next to worthless if the person doing the translation doesn't have a complete understanding of the subject and the culture of the language to which he is translating.

So this is why the method I use to teach hsing-i may seem different from other methods, perhaps less traditional than you have encountered before. This is because I believe it takes a Western mind to teach a Western mind.

Of the three internal styles of t'ai chi, pa-kua, and hsing-i, hsing-i has the strongest link with its martial arts background. T'ai chi, on the whole, is divorced from its original purpose, reduced to little more than gentle movements that have you breathing in time with the swaying of arms. This is great for relaxation and circulation, but it is criminal in regard to the real potential of the system. Reducing t'ai chi to this is like using a Ferrari Testarossa to go to the market once a week for groceries.

Thank God for masters like Erle Montaigue of the World Taiji Boxing Association. Montaigue teaches the internal systems for the purpose for which they were originally designed: the generation of effortless power by uniting the mind with the body for a specific application. The internal arts have the same grace and precision as a sport such as golf. But rather than attempting to get a little white ball into a hole, the purpose in hsing-i is to overcome an adversary with grace, power, and calmness. With these qualities in place, the internal martial arts act as a great vehicle for personal growth. The type of personal growth that I am referring to is not the "touchy-feely" kind that was fashion-able in the 1980s, but the growth that leads to action and taking responsibility for all one's thoughts and movements. When this type of growth takes place, an individual can achieve truly amaz-ing feats of learning, building success and happiness for them-selves and those around them. With these qualities in place, faith and spiritual awakening occur by themselves. The concepts of personal power have been taught through the '80s and '90s. With hsing-i these concepts progress from the realm of a good idea into a reality.

It is a sobering task to be faced with putting down on paper more than 20 years of study and discovery. I have realized in the process that so much cannot be expressed in words. A feeling for the art has to occur in your body. It is about the movement and the coordination of energy in the body, and it has to be experienced to be understood.

Rather than attempting to teach forms in a book, I have broken the forms down into their components. Greater skill can be obtained by developing the understanding and coordination of these parts. Practicing anything without understanding is very limiting, since you never develop the flexibility required to use it in real life.

1

Basics of Hsing-i

Hsing-i is famous for its raw power and hitting force. Yet, in a strange way, it is still very subtle in its application. One of the most interesting things about hsing-i is the calming effect produced through practice of the hand techniques. My teachers of Chinese medicine tell me that each technique stimulates a pair of organs in the body. This stimulation brings about harmony and health. These same teachers have told me that hsing-i is the most effective way to bring about this stimulation. It is difficult to comment on this as there is no empirical way of measuring it.

To better understand the underlying concepts of hsing-i, we can begin by looking at the meaning of the name. Roughly translated the word "hsing" means "form" and "i" means "of the mind," or "of ideas." Hence, we know it is a system that incorporates the mind as well as the body. I like to think of it as the body being used to express thoughts. This "form of the mind" can be thought of as a martial arts system that considers how a human being learns.

The intent of training in hsing-i is to reach a point where the conscious mind is blank. There is no real thought, just a sense of peace. All the information is stored in the subconscious mind, waiting for the right moment to be released. At the appropriate time, the lines, strategies, and maneuvers just "happen," as if by themselves.

The Internal Martial Arts Academy's aim is to look beyond the traditional explanations of the techniques, making it possible to learn why things were taught the way they were. This, in turn, makes it possible to change tradition if it has become so formalized that it has lost its relevance. To this end we have changed some of the animal forms to suit this more pragmatic approach to the internal arts. In addition, we teach personal development, concepts of traditional Chinese medicine, massage, and meditation, as these are all part of the process.

Another factor to consider when studying hsing-i is its close relationship with other martial arts systems. It can be described as the son of t'ai chi and the brother of pa-kua. To study one is in part to study the other two.

T'ai chi is the mother of Chinese systems and philosophies. T'ai chi is a symbol of the building blocks of the universe.

Pa-kua is a physical expression of the "I Ching" or "Book of Changes." It relates to heaven and the future and describes the system of divination.

Hsing-i is the physical expression of the wu hsing, the five elements that describe the workings of earth and are the foundations of Chinese medicine. There are two schools of hsing-i today, the school of the five elements and the school of the 12 animal forms. In this book we will deal with the school of the five elements.

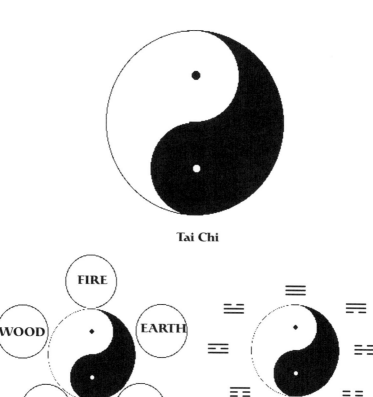

Tai Chi

Wu Hsing
The foundation of hsing-i

8 Trigrams
The foundation of pa-kua

Hsing-i's history can be traced back to the Sung Dynasty
(960 – 1279 A.D.) in China. It was developed by General Yue Fei,
who had formerly trained in Shaolin Temple Boxing and t'ai chi.
He trained his own men through a system that was a marriage of
these two disciplines. The locals in the area of Yue Fei's fighting
forces would say, "Easier to move the mountain than Yue's men."

You may ask, if t'ai chi is the ultimate martial arts system and
philosophy, why study hsing-i? There are several reasons. T'ai
chi's complexity can be overwhelming to the beginner. Hsing-i,

with fewer movements or variations, acts as a good stepping-stone to t'ai chi. Hsing-i is referred to as the link between the external arts and the internal arts and maintains all of the internal qualities of t'ai chi. Finally, Western people are more goal-oriented, whereas Eastern people are generally more process-oriented. Hsing-i is very goal-oriented, with a grading system and an organized system of steps, while t'ai chi relates to the process as a whole.

I have mentioned that hsing-i is an internal martial art. The key difference between internal and external martial arts is the level of relaxation and, consequently, the levels of muscle activity. In an internal system the level of relaxation is much greater than in an external system such as karate. Muscle performance becomes more efficient when the muscles start from a state of relaxation as opposed to tension. It is easier for a muscle to go from relaxed to contracted than from contracted to relaxed to contracted again. Energy consumption is also lower in the internal arts for the same reason.

Differences between internal and external are indicated by muscle physiology and neurology. As we train the body and, more specifically, the muscles to do only what we want them to do, the body works more effectively and a lot faster. Since there are fewer choices to be made, there are fewer decisions, and consequently reaction times are shorter.

A common myth about the internal arts is that they are soft or yielding. This is true to a point and not true at the same time. The external arts use muscle power to generate the hitting force from an established position of balance. Hsing-i, on the other hand, uses gravity and body mass to generate most of its hitting force, with the muscles being used to maintain structure to transfer that force to its target. Because of this there is little need for stance in the traditional sense.

Since the feet are not required to stay in the hitting position, they are free to be used for establishing safety or inflicting damage. Be aware, however, that during the moment a foot leaves the ground to hit an opponent it is not possible to find safety. It takes two feet to find safety and two feet to deliver a kick. You can kick and find safety at the same time only if you have four feet.

Hsing-i body positioning starts with the pi chen (pronounced pee-chen) stance. This position will be explained in detail later. Hsing-i also utilizes dual-hand movement. Each movement of the body is fluid and involves every part of the body. There are no block/hit-type motions. All actions are both a hit and a block at the same time.

One way of looking at hsing-i is to think of yourself developing three different skills at the same time: targeting, hitting, and triggering. You could think of them as different parts of a gun: sights, barrel, and trigger. The sights are the concept of having your centerline facing your opponent's center of mass at all times. The barrel is the five elements and stepping, which is the part that produces the power. The trigger is the mental programming of the exact moment to release the right element. This partnership of concepts and techniques works together beautifully.

Within each description of the five elements the trigger is described in detail. For the sights we have the information in this chapter.

Remember that you can have a huge cannon, but with faulty sights or no trigger it is just plain luck if you hit the target. Many martial arts schools spend enormous amounts of time just developing cannons. Hsing-i also develops a formidable arsenal of techniques, but the magic is in how it is put together.

Center

The most important thing to remember when training in hsing-i is center. At all times you face the opponent's center of mass. You may step past him, but your chest will always be directed toward him. If you are behind him your chest will be facing the middle of his back. The reason for this is simple: with your chest facing the opponent, defense or attack can be launched at any moment. It's as if you have a laser implanted in your chest that points directly forward. As you see your attacker your aim is to always have that laser pointed directly toward the middle of what you can see. So if the attacker is facing you directly the laser will be pointing to the middle of his forehead, chin, throat, heart, belly button, and groin (position A). If you

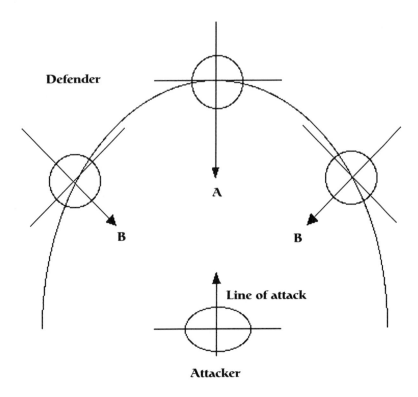

Defender

A

B   B

Line of attack

Attacker

now step to the side (position B) your targets will change to the side of the head, chin, throat, ribs, hip, outer knee of the closer leg, and inner knee of the other leg.

Footwork

There is really only one stance in hsing-i: pi chen. All the footwork is about stepping and transferring of mass from one point to another.

Every hand movement involves footwork. Consider the footwork as a way to establish direction to either evade or strike. The transition from one step to another should be done as smoothly as possible. Your head should stay on the same plane, with as little sideways motion as possible. At no time do you have stepping that you cannot hit from. Each step flows automatically into the next.

Power Generation

The majority of martial arts systems develop power through a rotary action of the upper body. This rotation starts by planting the feet on solid ground. Power generates through the rotation of the hips and up to the shoulders, where the rotary force is transferred to the arms and then finally to the fists.

A martial artist using rotation to generate power can use only one hand at a time for hitting. Enormous amounts of energy are required to drive the rotation to speed, and just as much energy is required to stop the strike if it misses its intended target.

One major point that must be considered here is that, since all hitting of this nature comes from the ground, the moment the hitter braces his feet he tells his opponent his next move. It is like having to lay foundations every time you want to hit and then having to lift the foundations and place them down again on moving to the next hit. This becomes very time-consuming and impractical against more than one attacker. It has been my experience that this usually gets the inexperienced practitioner of martial arts into trouble with his attacker.

Hsing-i uses the body's mass rather than its muscle to develop power. Put very simply, hsing-i could be described as the art of throwing your body at the attacker. This is the reason formal hsing-i has a lot of stamping—not only do we throw ourselves at the attacker, but at the ground as well.

Gravity is a pretty impressive force. It acts on a body every moment of the day, every day of our lives. I weigh around 80 kilograms (176 pounds). Allowing gravity to act on that mass for as little as a quarter of a second can develop enormous amounts of downward force. In order to gain access to this force, all one has to do is learn to relax or fall to the ground for the right quarter of a second. If you have any doubts about this, try having someone drop a bag of cement mix from just above your open arms. You will be surprised at how much force can be generated in such a short distance. Even when you are ready for the weight, it is next to impossible to hold. Two things to learn from this test are that not a single muscle is used to generate the force, just mass, and that most people are considerably heavier than a bag of cement.

For those of you who might be thinking, "Great! I don't have to exercise to be powerful," this is, unfortunately, not the case. The real magic of hsing-i is the way it redirects available force into a forward direction, and for this magic to occur, you do need toned, responsive muscles.

Dual-Hand Movements

With the chest aimed squarely at the opponent at all times, both hands can be used simultaneously. The force that we have been generating with the aid of gravity can now be put to good use. One hand acts as a defensive block or parry, and the second hand delivers the strike. The fact that two hands are in play at one time means that we are at least 50 percent faster than our rotary-based martial arts cousins. The speed and power of the dual-hand movements have to be seen to be truly appreciated.

I saw a vivid demonstration of this power when I was training in Taiwan. One of the senior students hit a junior student in an unnecessary show of force. This senior had been hitting junior students for a while, and this was the final straw. The master of the school witnessed the hit and asked the senior student to strike at him. At this point the senior knew he was in trouble and struck with considerable force. The master's hand dropped no more than six inches onto the oncoming forearm. The result was a sickening crunch, with the web between the senior student's right thumb and index finger ending up resting in his right elbow as he rolled around the floor in pain. I never saw the senior student again, but I will always remember the strike. If the master's second hand had come into play, it would have been all over for the student.

Hsing-i's aim is never to force an attack, but to follow a peaceful path at all times. However, when faced with a choice between life and death, its choice is always life.

In the West we have a notion of fair play—right and wrong—to the point that if you fight with all your might and lose there is still honor in it. If you follow the rules, we're told, you will eventually win. This is fine for the movies and storybooks, but the reality of life and nature is very different. In the animal world there is rarely a second chance. As a tiger selects her next kill, she will go after the old, the sick, or the very young. She knows that every time she hunts there is a chance that she may be injured. If that injury stops her from hunting, she and her cubs will die. Hsing-i and t'ai chi are expressions of the observations of natural order. There is no right or wrong as such—just the instinct for survival.

I learned another important lesson many years ago when I had the privilege of training in eido, or classical Japanese sword drawing. The master I trained under was an elderly gentleman the local police station in Tokyo had brought in to train its officers in swordplay. After all the training in kata, the master finished his training with me with one sentence: "Wait till the last moment before drawing your sword and you will be guaranteed your best chance of victory." It took me years of training to grasp the importance of what he was giving me as a parting present. In short, your waiting till the last possible moment forces your attacker to commit to his attack. As he continues his attack, his skill level remains constant, and his lines of movement and force are both continuous and easily read.

The magic of hsing-i occurs when the mind is calm and the attacker's oncoming move triggers a response at an instinctive level. Each of the elements has its own trigger. Once the trigger is pulled, the single element fires like a gun. If the elements are strung together, then your movements become like a machine gun. When practiced properly, the first three elements can be executed with full force in less than a second. It is necessary to practice this type of hitting on a dummy to appreciate the real power of hsing-i. If you practice on your classmates, you will be guaranteed to have a low turnout for the next training session.

In the section on the five elements we will look at how this works in practice. In the section on footwork we will be looking at the development of power, using gravity and the structure of the body to transfer that power to the hands and feet. In my years of training, many martial arts teachers had taught me how to develop power for hitting and kicking to do damage. With the Taiwanese master's single hit to the senior's forearm, it dawned on me that I was not learning how to hit—I was learning how to kill with apparent ease. What also came to my attention was the responsibility that goes with such power.

2

Exercises

The main focus of these exercises is on developing enormous stability around the lower back, abdomen, hamstrings, buttocks, and the sides. The upper body is worked on, but only in an indirect way. Concentrating on developing strength in the lower torso could be thought of as developing a girdle of muscle that starts at the knees and attaches itself to the rib cage. The diaphragm is also an important muscle to develop. The exercises consist of sit-ups, back raises, side raises, push-ups, and squats.

Depending on your personal body development, changes may not come all at once. When I was in my 20s my arms always looked weedy compared to the strength and size of my legs. It was not until my 30s that my arms and shoulders developed to give me a balanced physique.

To increase leg strength relevant to hsing-i, I recommend a shock-loaded type of exercise for the legs. The best way of doing this type of training is by jumping down from a height of 3 to 6 feet and then immediately jumping up on a step of 2 to 3 feet. This not only increases leg strength, but also ensures that the speed of the muscle firing is also increased.

As you will come to expect of hsing-i, exercises are done in a specific way. They must be done in an almost jerky fashion. For example, when first instructing students to train in this way, I ask them to concentrate on the speed of the sit-up, not the distance covered. In the beginning many of the students lie on the floor and look as if they are having convulsions. The one thing that sports science has taught me is that as you train a muscle, so it will perform. To train muscles to contract quickly it is necessary to practice quick contractions.

One other thing I ask of students is that they change from one position to the next as quickly and smoothly as possible. Then the number of repetitions is up to them. If they can only do one of each set, great. If they can do half the set with good posture, even better.

A normal workout consists of one exercise from each of the categories listed below. This makes a set. The first set is made up of the easiest in each category. The second set is of the next level of difficulty. By the fifth set it is quite a challenge, as it works virtually every part of the body. As a cardiovascular workout it is also excellent. However, be aware it is a high-impact workout. People with lower back, bone, or heart problems need to check with their sports doctor or physiotherapist first.

SIT-UPS

Sit-up 1: Simple crunch. Start lying flat on your back. Attempt to touch your nose to the ceiling.

Sit-up 2: Elbows to the knees: With knees bent and hands on temples, raise your right knee and touch with left elbow and then alternate.

Sit-up 3: Hand to foot. Lie flat on your back, arms stretched out. Lift your left arm to the straight right leg and then alternate.

Sit-up 4: "V" sit-ups. Lie flat on your back, arms stretched out. Lift both arms to both feet in a "V" position in the air.

BACK WORK

Single leg raises

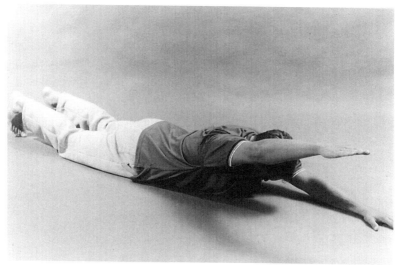

Arm raises

Back arches

SIDE RAISES (BODY ONLY)

Side raises

SIDE RAISES (BODY AND LEG)

Side raises

Military push-ups

Tucked push-ups

Shoulder down push-ups

Tiger push-ups

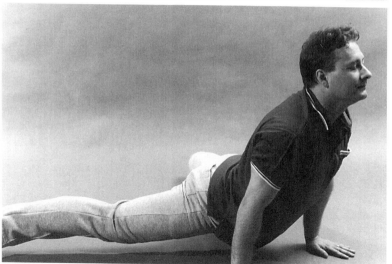

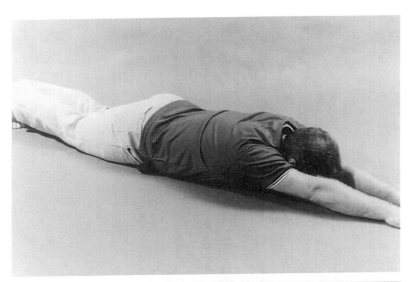

In-line press push-ups

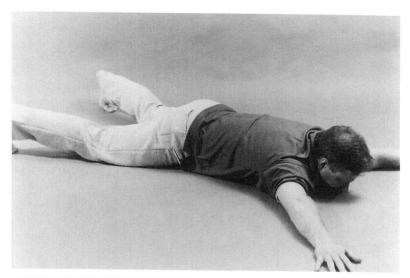

Star-press push-ups

Straight squat

 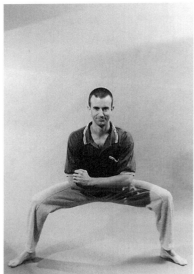

Spread squats

Jumping squats

Lunge squats

Crossover squats

STRETCHES

Side stretch 1

Hamstring stretches

Lunge stretch

Hip stretch

3

The Five Elements

Hsing-i is made up of
five sets of hand
movements or meth-
ods of coordination. These
movements are named after the
five elements of traditional
Chinese medicine. The magic
starts to appear when you realize that each element relates to
parts of the body, a system in
the body, an emotional state,
and pathways in the body
known as meridians. So when
the five elements are practiced
we are actually massaging our
bodies from the inside.

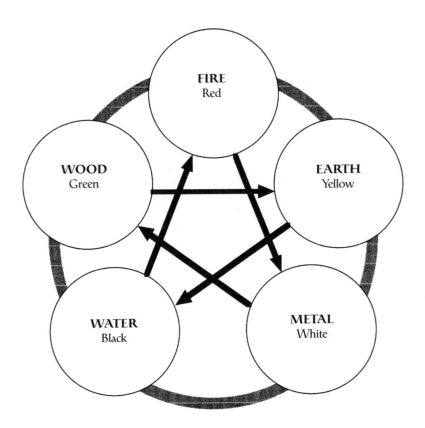

The five elements have a cycle of flow and control. This cycle is called the wu hsing. It is the basis of Chinese medicine and, more specifically, acupuncture. Above is a diagram of the wu hsing.

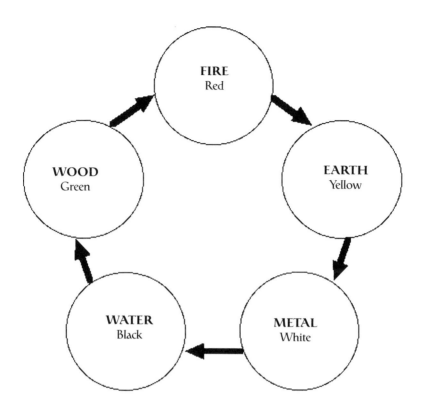

Sheng Cycle

The progression of metal, water, wood, fire, and earth is the sheng (meaning generative or creative) cycle. While the elements are always practiced in this order, it is interesting to note that some schools of hsing-i start the cycle with the fire element, while other schools teach metal first. I always start with the metal element as this was the first element taught to me. As to which element you start on, it is about as important as which foot you start walking with, the left or the right. Because it is a cycle you will end up at the beginning. When practicing the elements it is necessary to breathe deeply and concentrate on the internal organ that corresponds to the element you are practicing. This will be described later in the book.

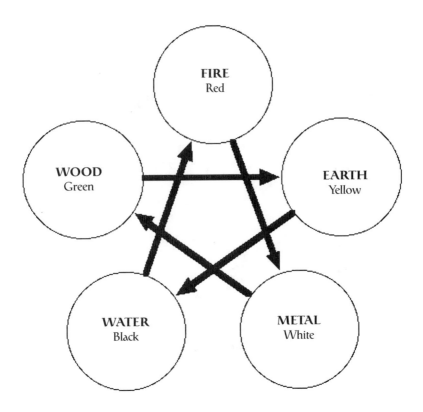

Ko Cycle

In the ko (controlling) cycle we have a relationship between elements. This relationship works in pairs. Metal controls wood, wood controls earth, earth controls water, water controls fire, and fire controls metal. The power of hsing-i lies in the application of the five elements, which are really just angles of attack. The moment an attacker uses an angle of attack, the appropriate element from the ko cycle is triggered and the defender continues according to the sheng cycle. All the attacker has to do is trip the trigger of the element and the element is fired automatically. No thinking or confusion, just an appropriate response.

For example, if an attacker uses a straight punch to the body, he is using a wood element. Metal controls wood, so metal is used against him. From metal the next elements are water and wood, so the sequence to be used against an oncoming strike to the stomach is metal, water, wood.

PI CHEN STANCE

Before you can start on the five elements it is necessary to learn the position of pi chen.

Taking a formal stance means taking an action. This action gives the attacker enormous amounts of information about you, such as your style, skill level, experience, and state of mind. So, by telling the would-be attacker these things, have you gained a strong defensive position? Generally not, because the first thing the attacker will be looking for is a way through your defense. He will find it because every strong stance has its weakness. So now you find yourself changing position to accommodate the oncoming attack. What you had gained was instantly lost, plus you have given away all that information and you have made two movements where only one was required.

To get around this situation we use the pi chen position. With both feet close together you are only a single step in any direction away from balance. Also, there is no illusion of strength, so you will have little desire to attempt to hold a position.

The desire to defend ground is one of the biggest problems new students face. It does not matter how good, strong, or fast you are, if you hold ground, your attacker knows exactly where to attack. With hsing-i we have to look at not giving away information and becoming as flexible in our positions as possible. But the idea of holding ground is embedded in our psychology very firmly. When young males fight as children it is about establishing dominance in the group. He who gets pushed back loses, we've been told, but in hsing-i we learn that no piece of ground is worth dying for.

- Stand with your head up, as if you are suspended by the hair on top of your head;
- tongue pressed to the roof of your mouth;
- palms open, facing forward, fingers together;
- leading hand level with the eyes, looking through the V shape of your leading hand;
- lower hand positioned in front of the tan tien, or sea of chi (a point found halfway between the navel and the pubic bone);
- shoulders relaxed;
- elbows relaxed and low;
- jaw closed and relaxed;
- feet and palms relaxed;
- shoulders slightly rounded forward;
- thumb held away from the body of the hand;
- knees, elbows, and wrist bent;
- neck and back held as straight as possible.

The most important part is to hold your spine as straight and tall as possible. Most people are not really aware of the shape of their spine when they stand. A simple test is to stand against a wall—if you can put your hand between the wall and your back, then you know you have some stretching to do.

There are two variations of the pi chen position, the more traditional left-foot-forward stance or the two-feet-together stance. Each has it advantages. The left-foot-forward stance is good for larger people or for fighting someone your own size, as the left foot can be lifted easily to stop the oncoming attack. The two-feet-together stance is great if the attacker is larger and more skilled. This will give you the opportunity to step left or right with greater ease. As I am only 5 foot 8 inches tall and most of my students are over 6 feet and physically stronger, I tend to use the feet-together stance often.

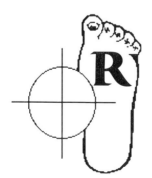

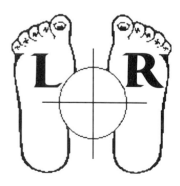

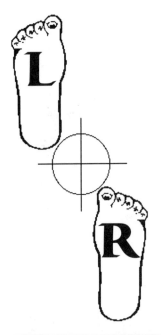

Common Problem

Too much weight is placed on the leading foot.

If you want to use the front foot for a stop kick or hsing-i kick, your center of balance has to be moved to the rear. Once your center of balance is moving it takes effort and time to stop it. If you come in contact with the attacker as your center is moving to the rear, it will be very difficult to hold your position, making it impossible to effect the technique.

Formal Start to the Pi Chen Position

Stand with your knees bent and your hands formed into fists held with the fingers touching in front of your body and just above the pubic bone. Your eyes are forward, and your breathing is relaxed and through the nose. Your head is pressed toward the sky. Your tongue is pressed onto the roof of your mouth. Your feet are flat on the ground with the heels touching.

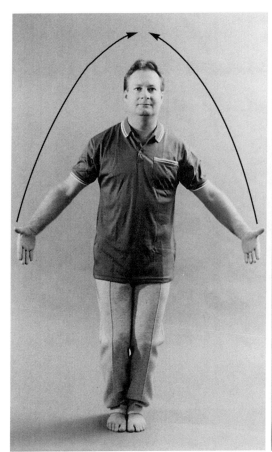

Hands start to separate

On the inward breath the hands open and separate to the side. The path of the hands creates a circle in the air, with the heart as the center. The elbows maintain the same angle as they travel along the edge of the circle.

Hands touch at the top

As the full inward breath is completed, the thumb and index fingers of each hand touch.

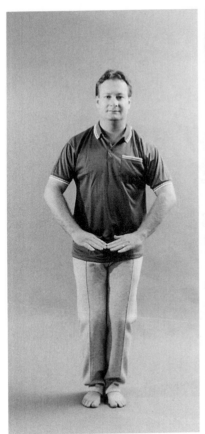

Hands press down

This touch triggers the outward breath as the hands travel downward in front of the body. As the outward breath is completed the hands, with the thumbs and index fingers still touching, come to rest over the tan tien.

Right hand presses forward

On the next inward breath the right hand presses forward as a fist. The feet are stationary, and the fist of the left hand gently presses into the left elbow to add support and structure to the center of the body.

Right hand clears the way
With the outward breath, the left foot lifts slightly and slides forward. The right fist opens and drops down the centerline of the body and the fingers extend, palm facing out. As this is happening the left hand lifts up the centerline of the body, palm facing the body.

The metal element corresponds to the lungs, which the Chinese call the masters of chi, or energy.

Mechanics

From the pi chen position your front hand drops onto the oncoming attack. Your second hand rises up along the centerline of your body, close to the chest, and is flung forward toward the attacker's head or chest so that both hands are pressing down, palms facing down.

Application

This is used against a straight strike to the chest or stomach or a front kick. Classically, metal is used against another person attacking with wood.

Trigger

The trigger for metal is the attacker's hand or foot entering under the forward on-guard hand.

Footwork

Most likely to be used with a front stamp, back stamp, or sawtooth step (45-degree step combined with a downward stamp). Each of these stepping techniques maximizes the use of gravity to heighten the effectiveness of the metal.

Left hand presses forward

On the next inward breath, your left hand presses forward as a fist. Your feet are stationary, and the fist of your right hand gently presses into your left elbow to add support and structure to the center of the body.

Left hand clears the way

With the outward breath, your left foot lifts slightly and slides forward. Your left fist opens and drops down the center-line of the body, and the fingers extend, palm facing out. As this is happening, your right hand lifts up along the centerline of the body, palm facing the body.

Both hands descend

You are still exhaling. The moment your right hand starts to drop, rotate both hands, pressing the palms forward onto the attacker. The front foot also drops onto the ground, amplifying the hit.

Right hand presses forward

On the next inward breath, your right hand presses forward as a fist. Your right foot steps forward, and your left fist gently presses into the right elbow to add support and structure to the center of the body.

Right hand clears the way

With an outward breath, your right foot lifts slightly and slides forward. Your right fist opens and drops down the centerline of the body, and the fingers extend, palm facing out. As this is happening the left hand lifts up along the centerline of the body, palm facing the body.

Both hands descend

You are still exhaling. The moment the left hand starts its drop, both hands rotate, pressing the palms forward onto the attacker. The front foot drops onto the ground, amplifying the hit.

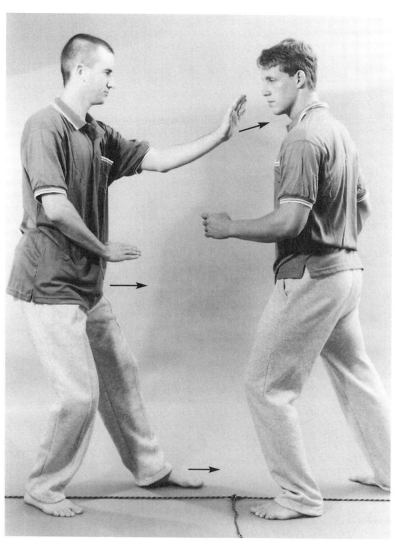

Application No. 1: Defense against an abdominal strike
Waiting for the trigger
As soon as the attacker's right hand enters under the left hand the metal response is triggered.

As the attacker advances with the strike, your left hand forms into a fist and is pressed forward to deflect the strike downward. Your left foot pushes forward strongly.

Your left hand pulls the attacker's arm to your tan tien. The palm of your right hand strikes down into the face of the attacker as your right foot stamps behind your left foot.

Application No. 2: Metal technique with front stamp
Waiting for the trigger

The attacker's right hand enters under your left hand. Your left hand simply drops palm down as your right hand lifts up along the centerline with the palm facing the body. The left foot lifts off the ground.

Both hands strike down at the same time. Your left foot hits the ground just a fraction of a second after your hands hit the attacker.

WATER

The water element corresponds to the kidneys.

Mechanics

Starting from the pi chen position, one hand descends along the centerline of the body as the other hand rises along the centerline of the body. Your leading hand deflects down, and your second hand strikes up to the face or throat.

Application

Water is used against a straight strike to the chest or stomach. Classically, water is used against a person attacking with fire.

Trigger

The trigger for water is a fist coming to the solar plexus.

Footwork

The most common footwork with this element is the back stamp, lunge, or advancing side step.

WATER TECHNIQUE

Start from a pi chen position with the left hand and foot forward, tongue pressed to the roof of the mouth, and breathing deeply into your abdomen.

Left hand presses forward

As you breathe in, your left hand presses forward slightly, rotating and forming into a fist with your thumb on the left so you can see your fingernails. Your weight shifts forward from 95 percent on the rear foot to even distribution.

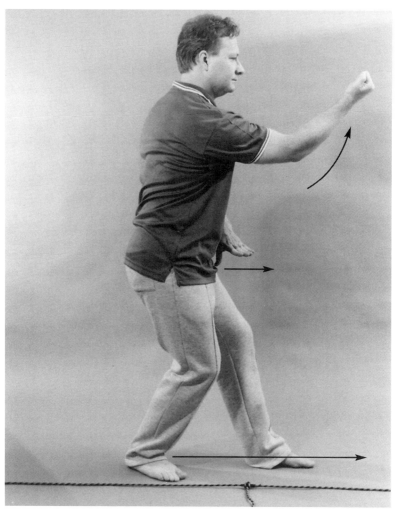

Water rises up

Your whole left arm then moves down toward the tan tien as your right hand comes up along the centerline toward the attacker's throat. Your right foot steps in front of the left.

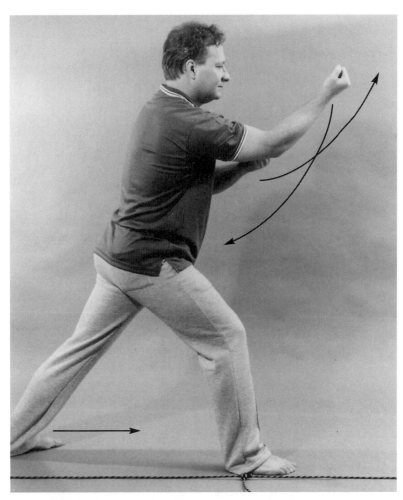

Right hand presses forward

As you breathe in, your right hand presses forward slightly, the fist still formed, with your thumb on the right so you can see your fingernails. Your weight shifts forward from 95 percent on the rear foot to even distribution.

Right hand grasps the arm or head
As you exhale, your right hand rotates, palm down, grasping and forming a fist.

Water rises up
Your whole right arm then moves down toward the tan tien as your left hand comes up the centerline toward the attacker's throat. Your left foot steps in front of the right.

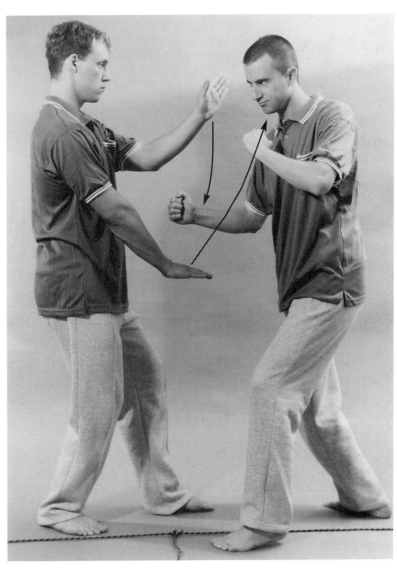

Application No. 1: Defense against a chest strike using water
The trigger for water is a fist coming to the solar plexus.

As the attacker advances with the strike, your left hand presses forward and downward to deflect it. Your body's weight shifts
forward onto the left foot, with weight now evenly distributed.

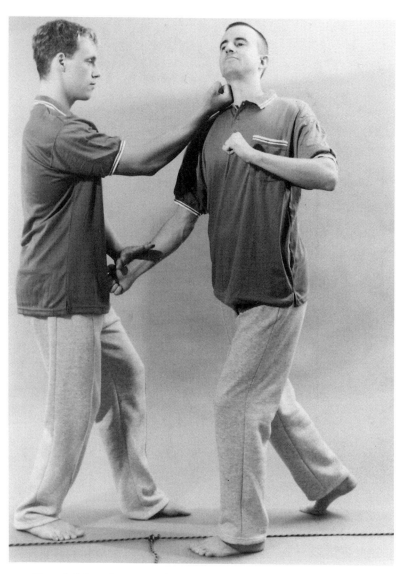

Your left hand presses down and pulls toward the tan tien. Your right arm pushes up along the centerline, crossing over the top of the left arm. The rear foot lifts off the ground and advances forward halfway to the front foot. The rear foot stamps down, driving the force up through the body, through the arms, into the fist and into the attacker.

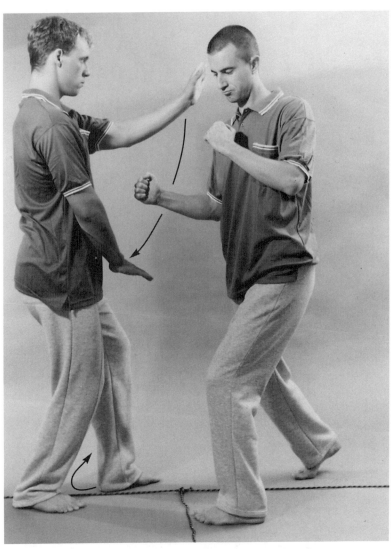

Application No. 2: Defense against a chest strike using a wave step
The trigger for water is a fist coming toward the solar plexus.
As the attacker advances with the strike, your left hand rotates
down, grasping the attacker's forearm. Your weight falls to the
right front at an angle of 45 degrees. This fall is caught by your
right foot, allowing you to fall off the attacker's line.

With your hand still in contact with your attacker's arm, guide it downward to your tan tien. Your right arm pushes up along the centerline, crossing over the top of your left arm. Your left foot now touches the heel of your right foot.

WOOD

The wood element corresponds to the liver.

Mechanics

Starting from the pi chen position, one hand descends, and one hand pushes forward. Your leading hand deflects down, and your second hand strikes to the lower abdomen.

Application

Use the wood technique against a straight strike to the stomach or crossing attacks from one side of the body to the other. Classically, wood is used against another person attacking with earth.

Trigger

The trigger for wood is any situation in which the attacker's hands or feet cross the middle of his body. An example would be the attacker's right hand reaching across to the left side of his body to execute a back-hand strike.

Footwork

The wood technique is commonly practiced with the feet-together stance, back stamp, wave step, and sawtooth step.

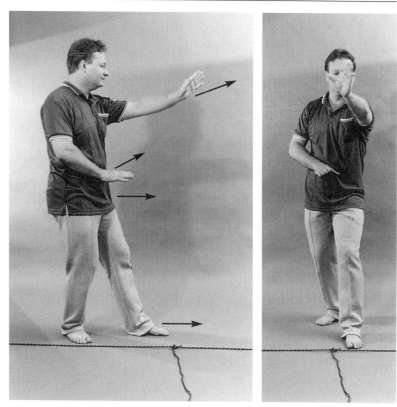

Start from the pi chen position with your left hand and foot forward, tongue pressed to the roof of your mouth, and breathing deeply into your abdomen.

Left hand presses forward

As you breathe in, your left palm rotates, and the hand presses forward. Your weight shifts forward from 95 percent on the rear foot to roughly even distribution.

Left hand grasps the arm

As you exhale, your left hand grasps and forms a fist. Your right hand also forms a fist—rotated, so you can see the thumb and no knuckles—in front of the tan tien.

Arms cross over

Your whole left arm now moves back toward the tan tien as your right hand comes up and over the left hand, driving forward and downward. The left foot, placed flat on the ground, drags the body forward, allowing the right foot to stamp down beside the left foot.

Right hand rolls over

As you breathe in, your right fist opens and the fingers extend forward. Your palm rotates counterclockwise and downward as the hand presses down. Your weight shifts forward as your right foot is placed forward.

Right hand grasps the arm

As you exhale, your right hand grasps and forms a fist. The left hand also forms a fist—rotated so you can see the thumb and no knuckles—in front of the tan tien.

Arms cross over

Your whole right arm now moves back toward the tan tien.
Your left hand comes up and over the right hand, driving forward and downward. Your right foot is placed flat on the
ground and drags the body forward, allowing your left foot to
stamp down beside the right foot.

Application No. 1: Defense against earth technique, wood with feet stamping together

The attacker's hand crosses the middle of his body to execute a back-hand strike.

As the attacker advances, your left palm rotates downward, catches the oncoming fist and presses down. Your weight shifts forward. Your left hand grasps the attacker's arm or wrist. Your right hand also forms a fist in front of your tan tien.

The attacker's right arm is pulled toward your tan tien as your right hand comes up and over the left hand, driving forward and downward to the attacker's tan tien. Your left foot is placed flat on the ground and drags the body forward, allowing the right foot to stamp down beside the left foot. Your fist drives deep into the attacker's center of balance, with all your advancing mass behind the fist.

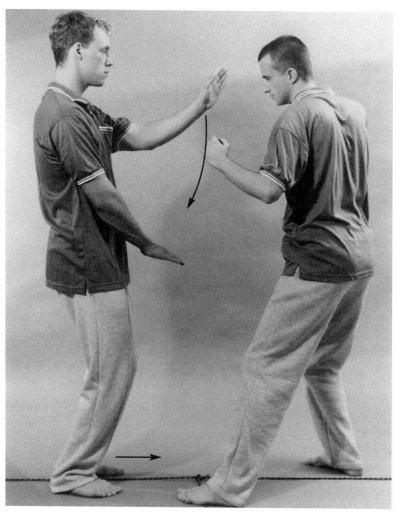

Application No. 2: Defense against right hook to the chest, wood technique with side step

As the attacker advances with a right hook, your left palm rotates downward, catches the oncoming fist, and presses down. Your body falls 45 degrees to the right and front.

This fall is gently caught with your right foot. Your center is focused on the attacker, but off to his side.

The attacker's right arm is pulled toward your tan tien as your right hand comes up and over your left hand, driving forward and downward to the attacker's tan tien. Your left foot is placed beside the right foot. Your fist drives deeply into the attacker's center of balance with your body weight dropping slightly.

FIRE

The fire element corresponds to the heart, which is said to be the emperor of the body.

Mechanics

Start from the pi chen stance. Raise both hands. Your leading hand deflects up, while the following hand hits just below the heart. The most effective stopping area is just below the sternum.

Application

Use the fire technique against a downward strike to the head. The upper hand is more of a deflection than a block. Classically, fire is used against another person attacking with metal.

Trigger

The trigger for fire is the metal element. This consists of any movement that comes over the top and back side of the hand when standing in a pi chen stance.

Footwork

The fire element can be used in conjunction with the lunge, back stamp, front stamp, and advancing side step.

Fire Technique

Start from a pi chen position with your left hand and foot forward, tongue pressed to the roof of the mouth, and breathing deeply into your abdomen.

Left hand lifts up to deflect

As you breathe in, your left palm rotates upward and presses to the front. Your right hand lifts from the tan tien and points directly at the solar plexus of the imaginary attacker. Step to the left at 45 degrees to the front. Point the toes of your left foot straight ahead. Your weight is evenly distributed.

Fire pushes forward from the right
As you exhale, your left hand moves toward your tan tien
and forms a fist. Your right hand also forms a fist and lifts up.
The right foot drives forward.

Application No.1: Defense against right hook to the head, fire with sawtooth step

The attacker advances with a right hook to the head.

Your left palm rotates outward so the thumb points to the ground, catching the hand or elbow of the attacker. Your right hand lifts from the tan tien, pointing with the fingers to the attacker's sternum. Step to the right at 45 degrees to the front. The toes of the right foot point straight ahead. The weight is evenly distributed between the feet.

As both your feet are brought together, your body weight drops slightly and is transferred to the hand and forearm, making the attacker jerk forward.

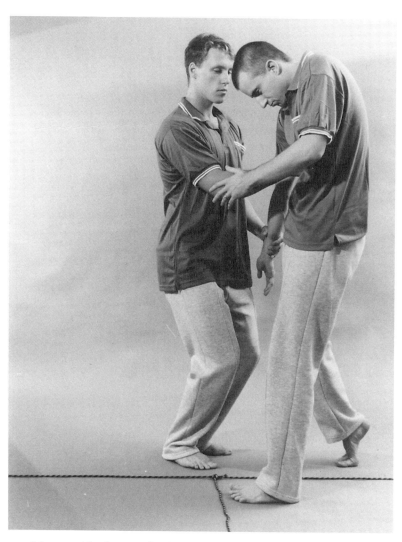

Now, with the attacker's weight coming forward, bring your feet together and drive your right fist into his solar plexus.

The earth element corresponds to the spleen.

Mechanics

Start in the pi chen position with both hands crossing. The leading hand deflects across the centerline of the body, followed by the lower hand. The lower hand hits to the side of the attacker's head or the torso.

Application

Used against a straight strike to the head or face. Classically, earth is used against another person attacking with water.

Trigger

While standing in a pi chen position with left hand extended, the element of earth is used as soon as the attacker's hands pass in front of the open palm of the presenting hand.

Footwork

Use with the side step, advancing side step, feet together, and lunge.

Earth Technique

Start from a pi chen position with your left hand and foot forward, tongue pressed to the roof of the mouth, and breathing deeply into your abdomen.

Left hand presses across

As you breathe in, your left palm pushes to the right. Your body falls to the left front at 45 degrees. This fall is caught by the left foot.

Right hand forms a fist

This position allows you to be off the attacker's line and still have your center on him. Your right hand forms a fist in front of your tan tien as your left hand gently pushes downward.

Right hand explodes forward

As you exhale, your right leg pushes forward as if toward the center of the attacker. Your right fist is pushed up on an arc toward the attacker's face.

Right hand presses across

As you breathe in, your right fist opens and pushes to the left. Your body falls to the right front at 45 degrees. This fall is caught by the right foot. The left hand forms into a fist in front of the tan tien, as the right hand gently pushes downward.

Left hand explodes forward

As you exhale, your left leg pushes forward as if toward the center of the attacker. Your left fist is pushed up on an arc toward the attacker's face.

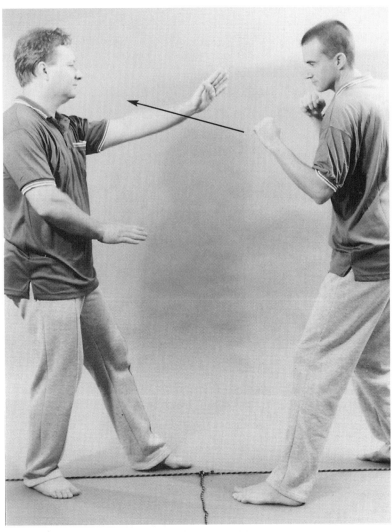

Application No. 1: Defense against left-handed strike to the head

Start by standing in the pi chen position with your left hand extended. As soon as the attacker's hands pass in front of the open palm of your presenting hand, the element of earth is used.

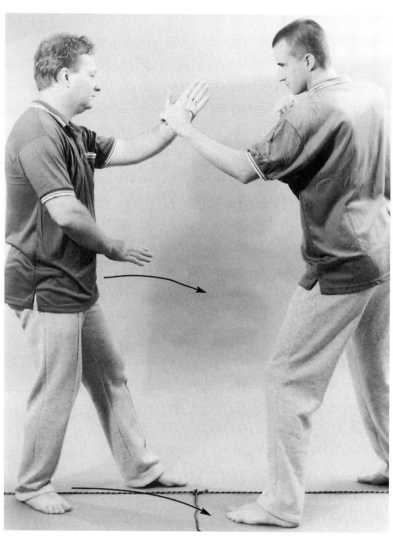

Your left palm rotates over the attacker's hand, catches the oncoming fist, and presses down. Your body falls 45 degrees to the right and front. This fall is gently caught with your right foot.

Your center is focused on the attacker and off to his side. Turn your body in front of the attack. Pull your left hand, still holding the attacker's wrist, toward your tan tien. Form a fist with your right hand in front of your tan tien.

Push forward with your right foot. With your right hand, arc forward and up to the attacker's jaw or throat.

Application No. 2: Defense against right-handed strike to the head

Start by standing in the pi chen position with your left hand extended. As soon as the attacker's hands pass in front of the open palm of your presenting hand, the element of earth is used.

Your left palm pushes to the right, catching the oncoming attack. Your body falls to the left front at 45 degrees. This fall is caught by the left foot. Your right hand forms a fist in front of your tan tien as your left hand gently pushes downward.

You are off the attacker's line and must have your center on him. Your right leg pushes forward, as if toward and between the attacker's feet. Your right fist is pushed up on an arc toward the left side of the attacker's face.

4

Footwork

Most of the footwork in hsing-i resembles an intended fall more than a driven step. This is where hsing-i differs from other systems. In most systems of boxing, the art of avoiding an oncoming blow depends on either stepping out of the way or planting the feet solidly and pulling the head out of the way. Hsing-i, on the other hand, keeps the feet close together and the knees bent. Avoidance is achieved by simply lifting a foot and falling in the desired direction. The maneuver is completed by driving the foot that was lifted into the ground. This launches us into the attack. It is amazing how much force can be generated and how much ground can be covered quickly in this way. An interesting point is that you can hit at any time through each step.

Giving in to gravity is, without a doubt, one of the most unusual experiences a new student of hsing-i has to go through. From the first moment of our walking life we fight for balance, and then in hsing-i we must learn to give it away in situations in which we think we should want absolute control. This does take a bit of getting used to, but with practice it becomes easier, then easy, then fun.

It is amazing how much speed you can develop this way. In some ways the speed is an illusion, as there are no tell-tale signs of muscle contraction to inform your opponent that you are about to jump out of the way. It will not register to him that you have already started the step, lunged, or changed your position until it is too late.

An easy way of trying this out is to stand with your knees bent and your weight evenly balanced between your feet. Then just lift one of your feet without changing your center of balance. It is amazing how little energy is used and how fast you can move off the spot when surrendering to gravity in this way.

The transition from one position to another should be as smooth as possible. Each step should flow automatically into the next step. Your head should stay on the same plane with as little sideways motion as possible. This may sound like a contradiction—keeping your head at the same level and falling at the same time—but it can be done if you learn the trick to it. As you fall you push with the rear leg, and, as a result, your head stays pretty much at the same level. This accelerates you forward at the same time.

THE LUNGE

The lunge closes the gap between you and the attacker, forcing him to recalculate the distance between the two of you in mid-attack.

Mechanics

The hands support each other, and the body is straight. It is not really a strike, as such. It is more like making yourself into a spear. The heel of the spear is thrust into the ground, and the attacker then impales himself upon the pointy end. Nearly all of the maneuvers of hsing-i will have a lunge in their footwork somewhere.

Application

Use the lunge during the initial attack. Even if the attacker has survived the first lunge, it is unlikely that his subsequent advances will have the same force or intensity.

Having been on the receiving end of such a lunge in my early days of training, I can vouch for its effectiveness. Both my feet came off the ground, and I landed flat on my back. The teacher at the time was being nice to me and used an open palm to the chest, as compared to a closed fist to the throat or jaw that is the usual practice.

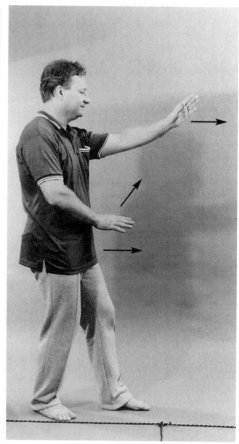

Weight Distribution

Weight is distributed evenly on both feet.

Start by standing in the pi chen position. This can be in the feet-together stance or with the left foot forward. The leading foot pushes forward strongly. The rear foot is flat on the ground and pushes strongly. The heel of the rear foot must stay on the ground.

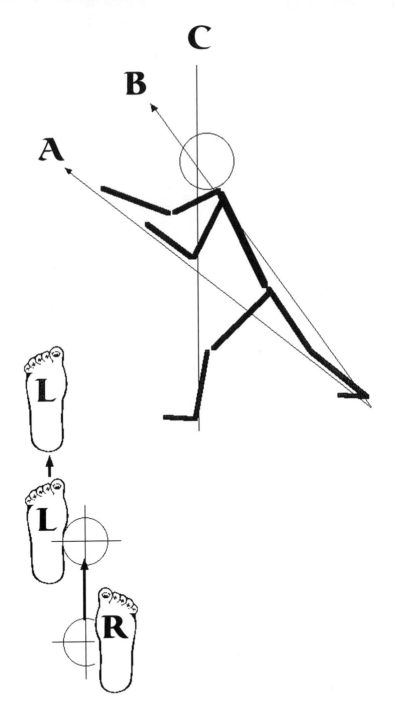

In the final position you will be leaning forward slightly. Use a mirror to check the angle between lines A and B and try to make it as small as possible. The knee of the front leg must stay above or slightly behind the foot (line marked C). Make your back as straight as possible.

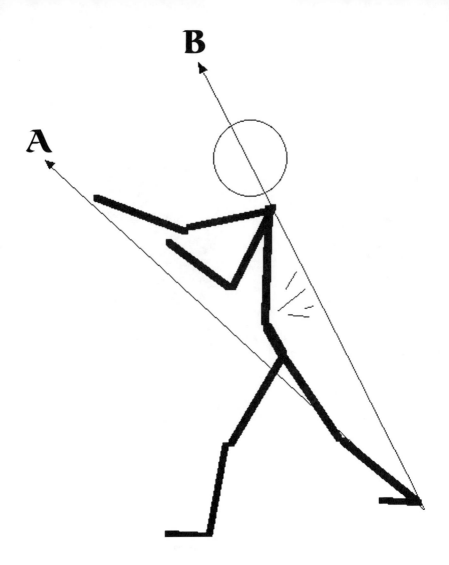

If you are too upright and the angle between A and B is too great, pressure placed on the leading hand can cause a strain in the lower back. You will also have to struggle to hold the attacker back. This is the indicator that you need to change the shape of your lunge.

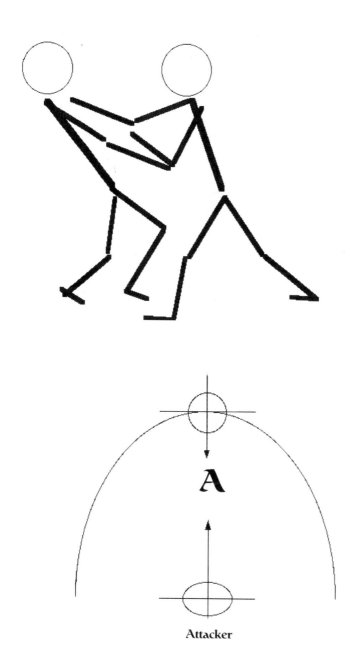

Attacker

Application 1: Straight lunge

This is a very strong technique. It is fast, simple to apply, and hard for the attacker to detect until it is too late. Remember to keep your hips and shoulders square to each other.

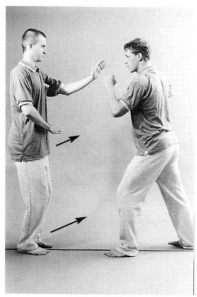

Application 2: Angled lunge

The major advantage of the back stamp is that it repositions your feet under you without shifting your center of mass.

Mechanics

To execute the back stamp, lift your rear foot quickly and place it down directly under your center of balance. The back stamp takes you from a long stance to a short stance in one step.

Application

This action prepares the practitioner for a lunge, front stamp, or side step. It can also be used as a hitting platform.

The advantage of the back stamp is obvious when facing a rushing attack. If you have your weight spread between your feet in a lunge position when the attack begins, it is usually necessary to move weight to the forward foot or back foot. As this happens the mass also travels. If you move forward, the attacker can easily choke the movement, leaving you no power or room to perform the desired maneuver. If you shift your weight to the rear foot, you'll have time and space to perform the technique, but you'll also make it easy for the attacker to continue the movement of your center of mass to the rear and knock you off balance. By moving your feet under you, you maintain balance and center. With this move, power can be generated forward with ease and speed.

Weight Distribution

Start with weight evenly distributed and finish with 5 percent of your weight on the front foot, 95 percent on the back foot. Your center of balance stays in the same spot.

The back stamp starts with a little hopping motion on your back foot. Then the front foot pulls the back leg forward. One way of thinking about this action is to imagine a balloon between your knees. Leave the front foot on the ground and hop with your back leg and squeeze your knees together in an attempt to burst the balloon.

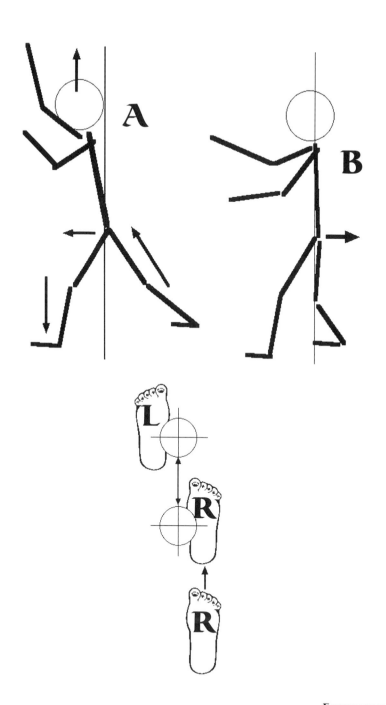

The major problem new students face with this step is the desire to push up with their back leg. This will push your center of balance forward, increase your height, and increase the weight on your front foot. These in themselves are not so bad, but then as you put the rear foot down, your center of balance is moved to the rear. This forward-and-back rocking motion effectively neutralizes the whole step, since you cannot hit forward and step back at the same time with power. The power of this step comes from the forward and slightly lower center of balance.

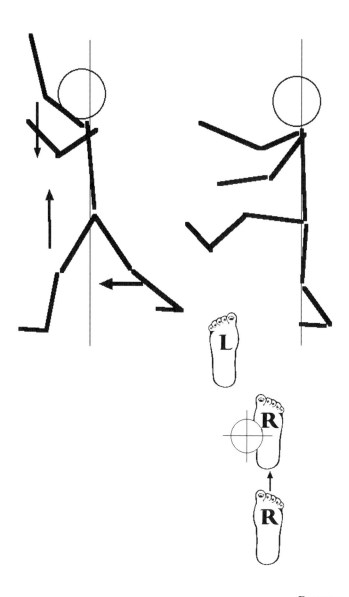

Application 1: Back stamp to establish a kicking platform
As the attack comes in, your rear foot hops to the center of balance. Your front foot kicks straight to the abdomen, knee, or the solar plexus.

FRONT STAMP

The front stamp is used to maximize the force of a strike.

Mechanics

The power of the hit is generated by using the mass of your leg as it travels toward the ground. The front of your leg, your abdomen, and chest all contract a fraction of a second before your foot hits the ground. The idea is to transfer the downward force of your leg into the arms.

Application

This is a very easy way to increase hitting potential dramatically. The amount of force is very impressive, especially when you realize that this force can be generated in a distance of a few centimeters. It is most commonly used with metal and wood techniques

Weight Distribution

Start and finish with 5 percent of your weight on the front foot, 95 percent on the back foot. Center of balance is stationary.

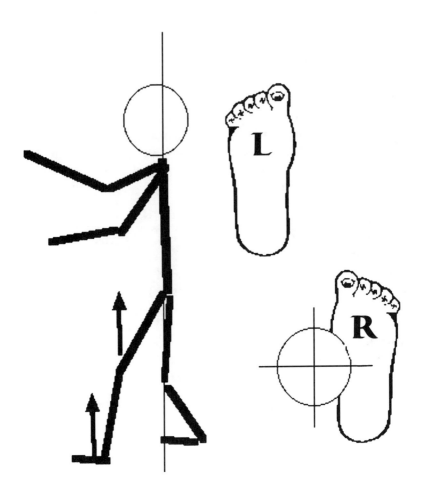

From your pi chen position, lift your leading leg. The center of balance is maintained.

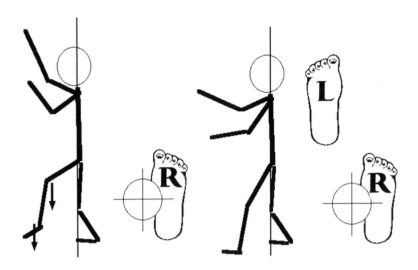

Drop your foot back to its starting place and drop your center of mass slightly.

Common Problems

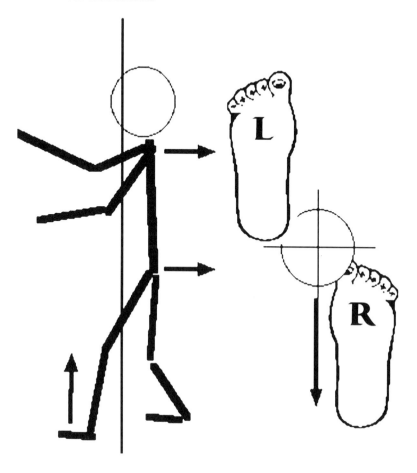

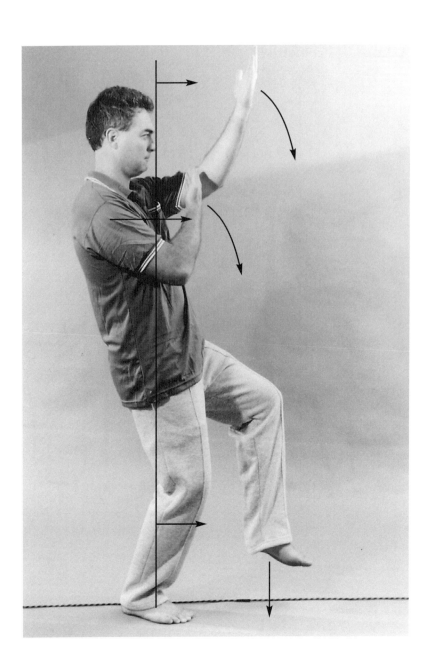

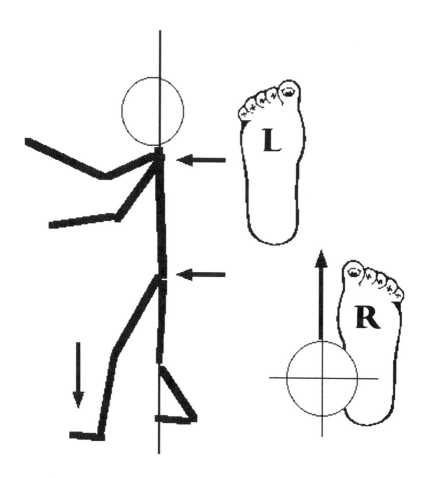

Start with the center of balance between your feet. As your front foot lifts off the ground, your center of balance is moved to the rear. To do this with speed, students commonly throw their shoulders back to compensate. If you are touched by the attacker on the upper body at this point, he can easily knock you backward.

As the strike is executed, your center and shoulders whip forward. The main problem here is that you tell the attacker exactly what you are doing. As you pull your head and shoulders backward, the attacker expects the next move to be forward, and it is. This maneuver also puts a strain on the lower back. Since your hitting force is being generated by the forward flick of the upper body, all your attacker need do is hold out a hand to stop you, and it is all over.

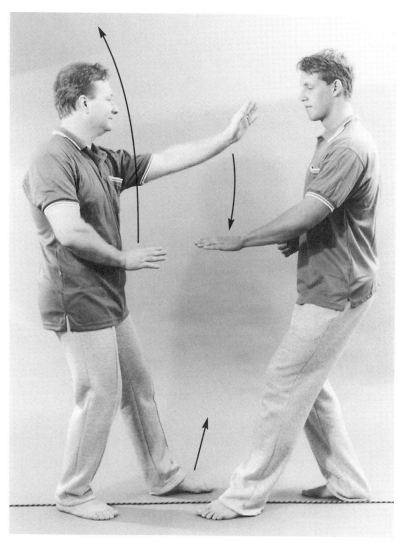

Application 1: Front stamp metal used against a strike to the stomach

Stand in your pi chen position, left hand and foot forward. As the attacker runs in, your job is to stay calm and wait for your trigger.

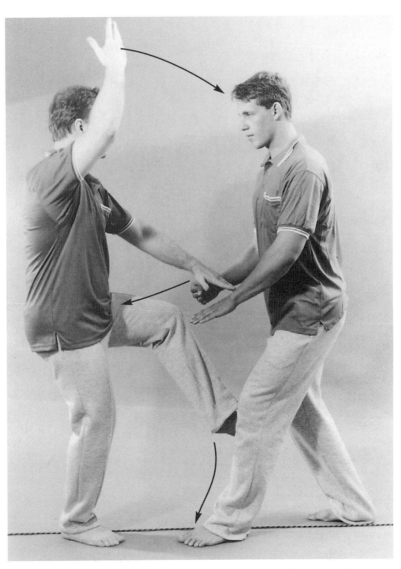

As the trigger point is reached, lift your left foot and drop your left hand onto his oncoming forearm. Your right hand is already loaded for the moment that your left foot starts for the ground.

The aim is to hit the attacker in the head or chest with your right hand just a fraction of a second before your foot hits the ground.

Application 2: Hsing-i kick, metal technique

As the attack comes in, your left hand drops onto the attacker, and your left knee lifts up.

As your hand comes into contact with the oncoming attack, your foot presses on to the knee of the attacker. When done correctly, the aim is to catch the attacker's leg in midstep. This will have a number of effects. It could break his knee, but usually it just drives his foot down to the ground, forcing him to take a short step. His center of mass is still traveling forward, making him lean forward into your defensive hand.

An attacker being hit with both the wood technique and the feet-together stepping pattern will have little chance of standing his ground. It is most likely that his legs will give way and his backside will hit the dirt.

Mechanics

The idea behind the feet-together position is to bring the head, shoulders, hips, and feet into one straight downward line. This will maximize the effect of the body mass falling to the ground. The step can be performed from a final lunge position or pi chen position.

Application

This stepping pattern is used for the elements that fall, namely metal and wood. It is most commonly used with wood, as the downward force of your mass has amazing effects when hitting the attacker's center of mass.

Weight distribution

If you are starting from a lunge position, weight is evenly distributed. If you are starting from a pi chen position, 95 percent of the weight is on the rear foot, and 5 percent is on the front foot. Finish with feet side by side, weight evenly distributed. Move your center of balance forward, directly over both feet.

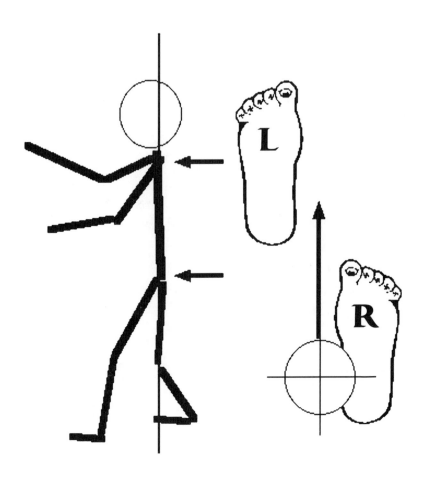

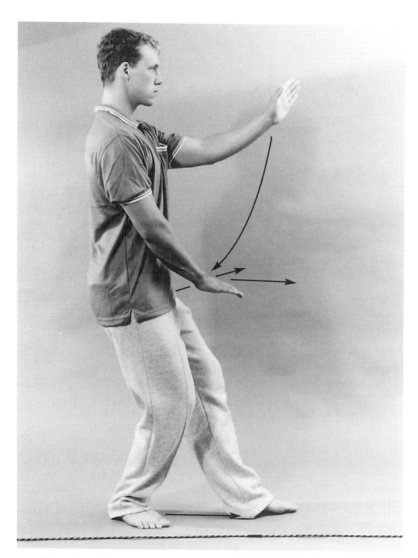

If starting from a pi chen position, the feet-together stamp is similar to a back stamp. The only difference is that here the feet start to move together at the point in which the back stamp would be finishing. There is the same motion as if squeezing a balloon between the knees and the same slight drop of the center of mass.

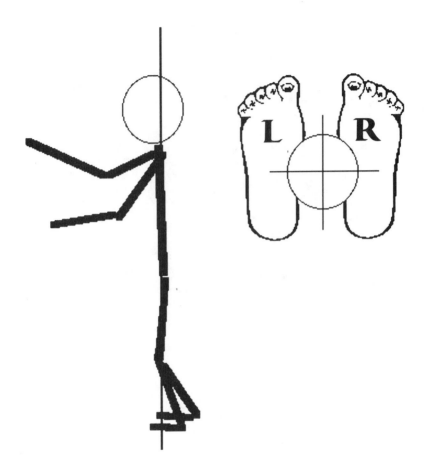

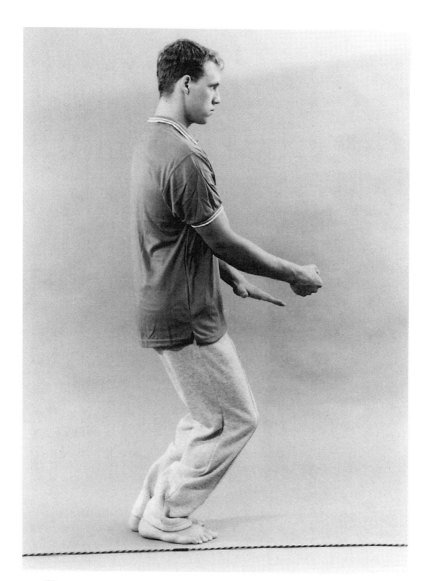

The most important thing to remember is to keep your elbow as close to the center line as possible. This will enable you to use the maximum force throughout the attack.

Correct Hand Position

Incorrect Hand Position

Common Problems

As your elbow comes away from the midline of your body, an enormous amount of muscle is required to deliver the strike. Because your feet are together, every inch that you are off center will have the effect of spinning you around. The end result is that the confidence to deliver the full potential of the strike is missing.

Another common mistake is the tendency to bend at the waist and not at the knees. Instead of hitting from the center, you are letting your abdominal muscles do all the work. It is also much easier to be pulled forward from this position.

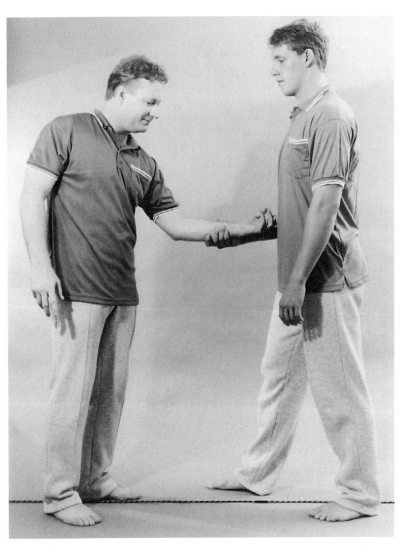

Application 1: Disruption of the attacker's balance using feet together

Your left arm or wrist is grabbed.

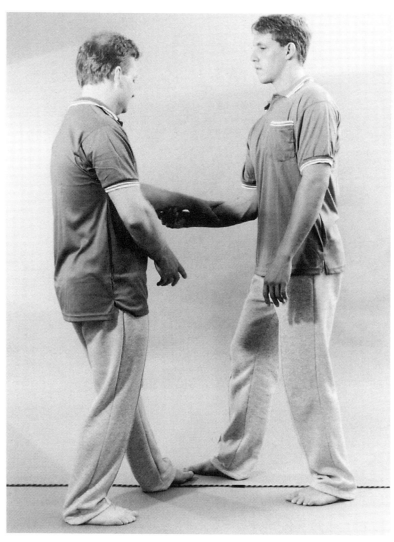

Rotate your center onto the center of attack.

Your right foot moves level with your left. Your right hand presses down on the attacker's right elbow. Your center of mass is dropped as your feet move together. You may dislocate the attacker's elbow or shoulder with this move. At the very least, the attacker's right knee will bend so you can take him to the ground.

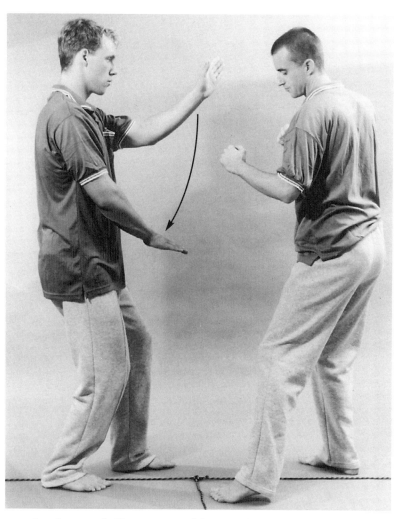

Application 2: Disruption of the attacker's balance using feet together

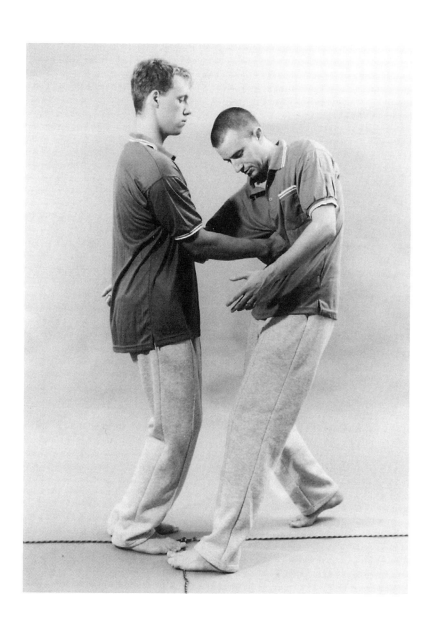

SAWTOOTH STEPPING

This side step allows you to step off the line of power and at the same time maintain the optimum line for striking.

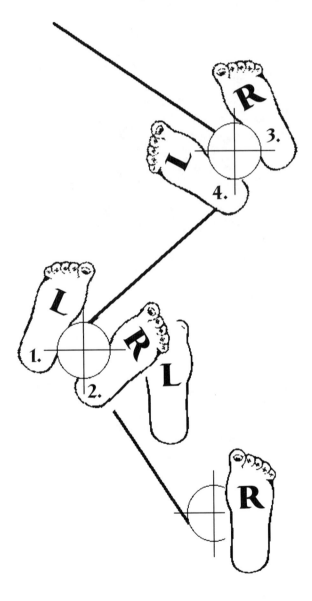

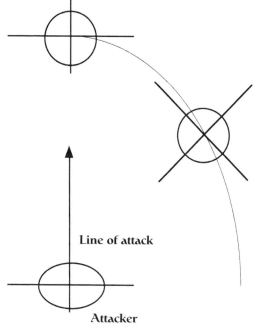

Defender

Line of attack

Attacker

Mechanics

This step has the mechanics and applications of the feet-together step, but with a motion to the side. It is named for the pattern made as you practice it across a room. The whole purpose of this step is to come off the line of attack and establish a position of strength from which to hit, drag down, or launch an attack.

Application

Apply this move when the power of the incoming charge is too great to be handled easily. This technique gets interesting at the point in which the feet come together and the body weight is traveling toward the ground. It is at this point that you want to be in contact with the attacker, either with the back of your fore-arm across his incoming strike—a metal or wood technique—or just holding his arm. Your aim is to drive the attacker to the ground with this action. Again, because of gravity and mass, this is a very impressive maneuver.

Weight distribution

Start from a pi chen position. Weight is distributed 95 percent on the right foot, 5 percent on the left foot. Then there is a shift as your left foot moves to the left with a 45 degree turn of the centerline of the body. Weight remains 95 percent on your right foot, 5 percent on your left foot. Center of balance moves from the right foot to between the two feet.

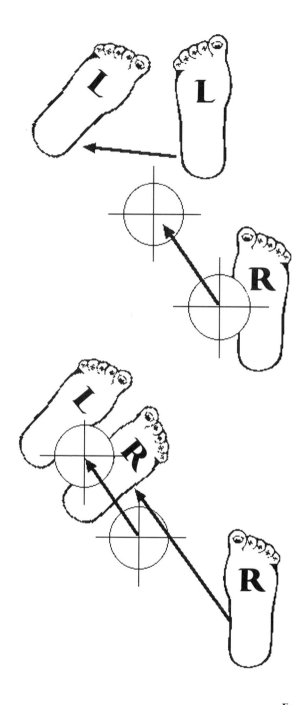

The right foot slides parallel to the left. Weight is evenly distributed on both feet. The center of balance moves from between the feet to the left foot. At this point there is a stamp downward. It is as if the feet are used to stop your fall to the ground.

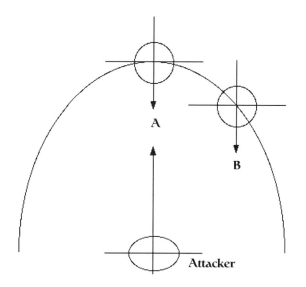

A

B

Attacker

Common Mistakes

Instead of the center being turned to face the attacker, the center is aimed off to the side. This usually happens because the left foot, instead of turning inward, steps straight ahead. This in turn produces a one-two movement—one to get off the line and two to hit. This takes time that you frequently will not have. The attacker will be on top of you before you can make the shift. Your leading foot should be pointed at the attacker's center of mass the moment the foot hits the ground.

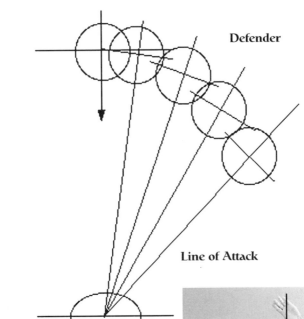

Defender

Line of Attack

Attacker

Remember that your center has to point at the attacker through every part of the side step. This allows you to defend or hit from any part of the step.

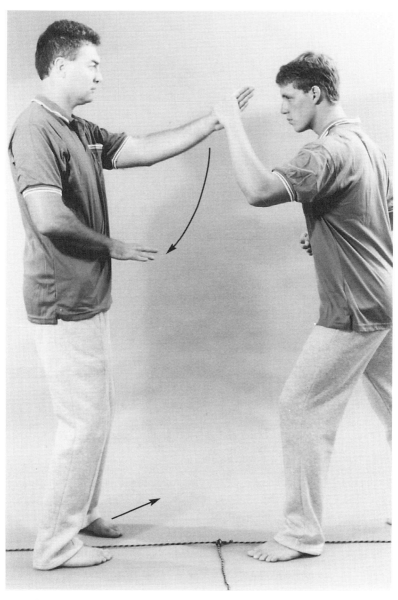

Application 1: Sawtooth step with wood technique
The attacker's hand triggers the element and step.

Your body weight falls to the right. Your left hand drops onto the oncoming attack from the attacker's right hand, grasps it, and starts the pull to your tan tien.

As your feet come together, your left hand finishes pulling the attacker toward your tan tien. By doing this, his balance is disrupted. Your right hand strikes forward into his center.

WAVE STEPPING

As with sawtooth stepping, the wave step allows you to move off the line of power and at the same time maintain the optimum line for striking. There is an incredibly fast transition of weight and line of force. It will also close the distance between you and your attacker very quickly.

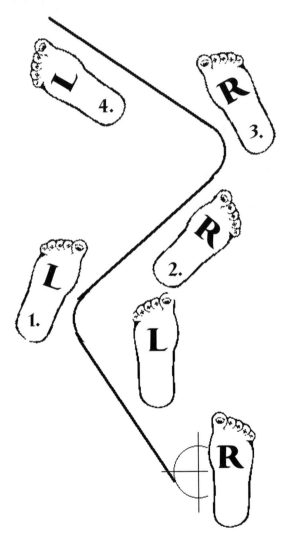

Mechanics

Wave stepping and sawtooth stepping are very similar. They have the same starting position, the same finishing position, and even the same foot positions. The only difference is that in wave stepping, your right foot swings straight past your left foot. There is no stamp or stopping in the middle of the maneuver. Like sawtooth stepping, it is named for the pattern that you make as you practice up and down the room.

Application

Again, this is a move to apply when the power of the incoming charge is too great to be handled easily. The most important thing to remember is that as the feet change position, it is also necessary to turn your center around so it faces your attacker's center at all times (see figure below). The arrow indicates the need for your center to always be pointing in the right direction.

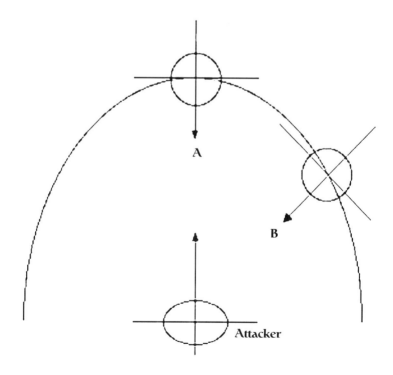

A

B

Attacker

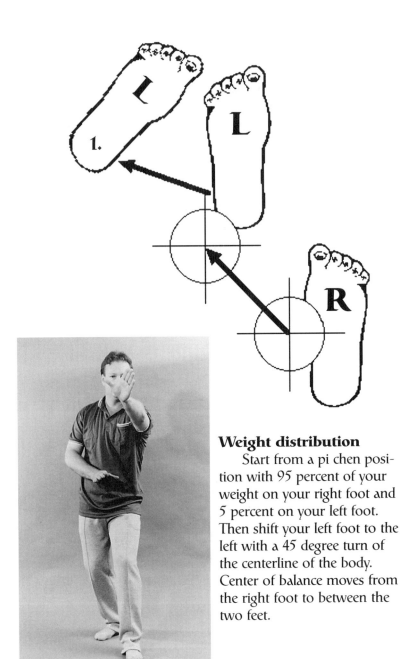

Weight distribution

Start from a pi chen position with 95 percent of your weight on your right foot and 5 percent on your left foot. Then shift your left foot to the left with a 45 degree turn of the centerline of the body. Center of balance moves from the right foot to between the two feet.

Your right foot slides parallel to the left. All your weight is on your left foot. This is where it differs from the sawtooth step. Your center of balance moves from between the feet to the left foot.

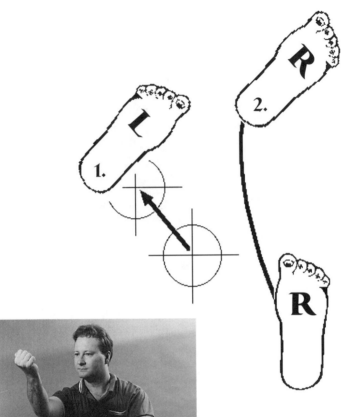

Your right foot pushes forward as the strike is performed. Weight is 95 percent on your left foot, 5 percent on your right foot. Your center of balance stays in the same spot.

Common Mistakes

As with the sawtooth step, the most common mistake is allowing your centerline to swing off the attacker's center.

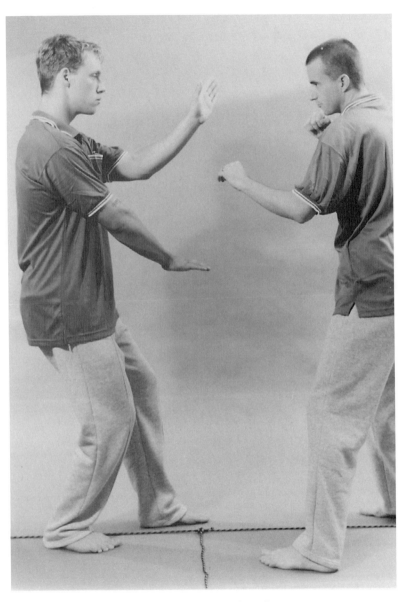

Application 1: Wave step with earth technique

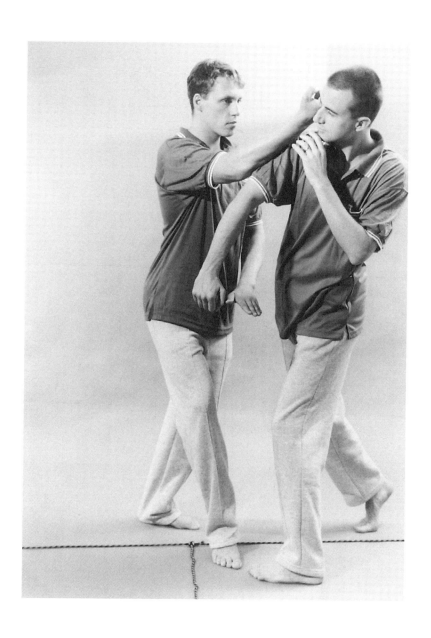

5

Combining the Elements

It is in the applications that we start to see the real speed and power of hsing-i. The very quick hand exchanges combined with the forward press of the center of mass make this art just overwhelming. As we approach the applications, it is important to keep in mind that practicing form is a MUST. It is without doubt the single most important ingredient in all training. It teaches correct posture, line, muscle usage, coordination, and timing.

What follows are the applications of these forms in a practical setting. This where we bring all of the parts of the puzzle together, and this is where I have most of my fun. It could be that I am a little strange, or it could be that I realize that this is where it counts most of all. This is the point where you have an individual running at you attempting to harm you and you have to put it all together.

Now your breathing is calm, your mind focused and blank at the same time. You have practiced your forms to the point that they are second nature. As the attack occurs, the feet and hands work together. There is no time for fear, because this is the time to practice breathing in the moment. In most schools, the first thing the student does at the point of attack is hold his breath. In hsing-i this is where it is most important to breathe. Remember that the lungs are the masters of energy—stop them from working and you stop the flow of energy to the body. With reduced energy it is very likely that if you do come in contact with the attacker you will simply bounce off.

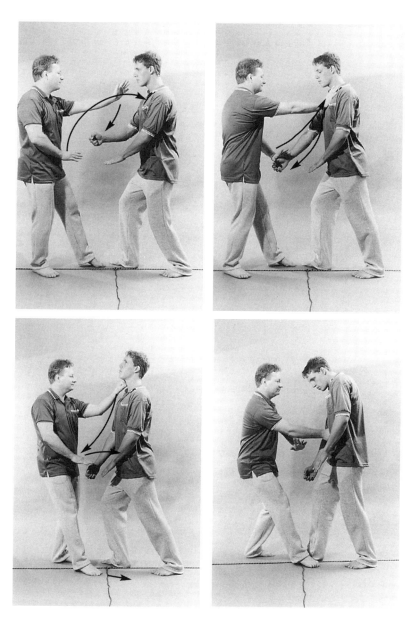

Metal/Water/Wood Sequence
Straight strike to the body

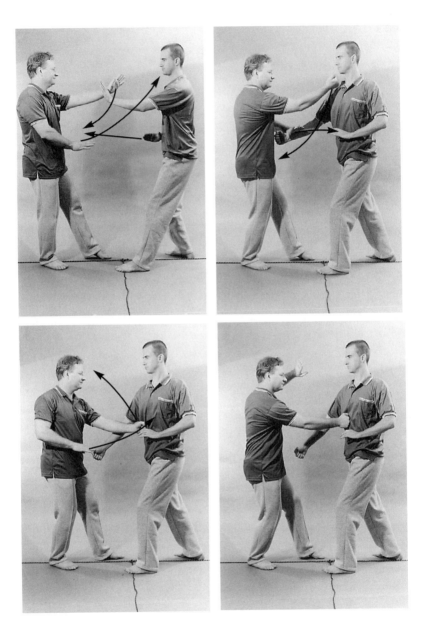

Water/Wood/Fire Sequence
Attacker advances with upper cut to the face.

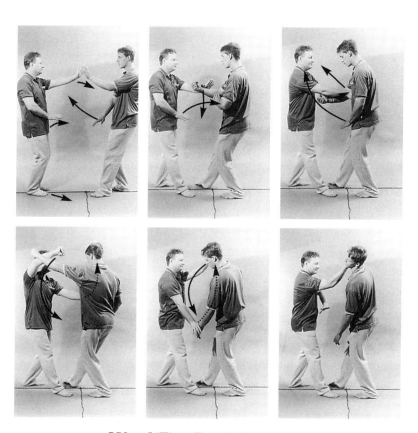

Wood/Fire/Earth Sequence

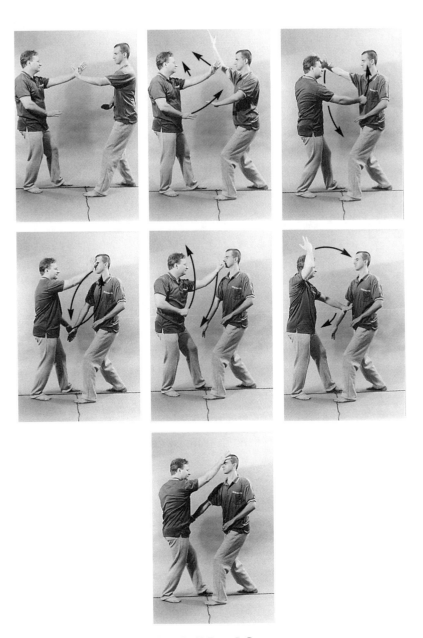

Fire/Earth/Metal Sequence

Earth/Metal/Water Sequence